World of Mammals

Elephants

by Xavier Niz

Consultant:
Carol Buckley
Executive Director
The Elephant Sanctuary
Hohenwald, Tennessee

Capstone
press

Mankato, Minnesota

Bridgestone Books are published by Capstone Press,
151 Good Counsel Drive, P.O. Box 669, Mankato, Minnesota 56002.
www.capstonepress.com

Library of Congress Cataloging-in-Publication Data
Niz, Xavier.
    Elephants / by Xavier Niz.
        p. cm.—(Bridgestone books. World of mammals)
    Includes bibliographical references and index.
    ISBN 0-7368-3717-5 (hardcover)
    1. Elephants—Juvenile literature. I. Title. II. Series: World of mammals.
QL737.P98N59 2005
599.67—dc22   2004015798

Summary: A brief introduction to elephants, discussing their characteristics, habitat, life cycle, and
    predators. Includes a range map, life cycle illustration, and amazing facts.

Editorial Credits
Erika L. Shores, editor; Molly Nei, set designer; Ted Williams, book designer; Erin Scott, Wylde Hare
    Creative, illustrator; Kelly Garvin, photo researcher; Scott Thoms, photo editor

Photo Credits
Digital Vision/Gerry Ellis, 1
James P. Rowan, 10
Minden Pictures/ZSSD, cover
Tom & Pat Leeson, 4, 6, 12, 16, 18, 20

1 2 3 4 5 6 10 09 08 07 06 05

Table of Contents

Elephants

Millions of years ago, many kinds of elephants roamed the earth. They lived on all of the seven continents except Australia and Antarctica. Today, elephants only live on the continents of Africa and Asia.

Elephants are the largest land **mammals** on earth. Like all mammals, elephants are **warm-blooded** and have backbones.

◀ Elephants are large mammals that live in Africa and Asia.

6

What Elephants Look L

Elephants are known for their lor
noses called trunks. Elephants use th
to touch, smell, and breathe.

Elephants have four teeth in the back
mouths. They have two in the front called
Tusks are used to dig for food and water.

Asian and African elephants have some
differences. African elephants are larger
than Asian elephants. An Asian elephant is
8 to 10 feet (2.4 to 3 meters) tall. An African
elephant stands 10 to 13 feet (3 to 4 meters) tall.

◄ Asian elephants have smaller ears than African elephants.

Elephant Range Map

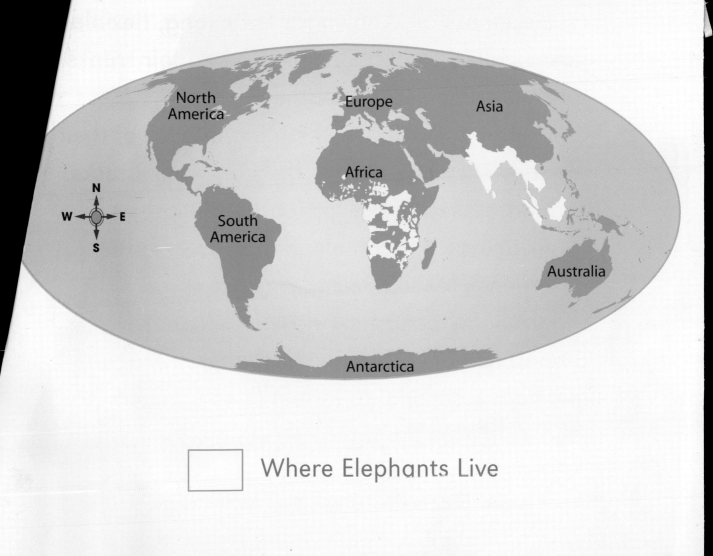

Where Elephants Live

Elephants in the World

African elephants live in central Africa. Asian elephants live in Southeast Asia, southern China, and India. Some Asian elephants are kept on farms. Farmers use them to carry heavy loads.

Most elephants live in national parks or other wildlife reserves. In these areas, it is against the law to kill elephants. Elephants roam the parks looking for food.

◄ Elephants live in Africa and Asia.

Elephant Habitats

An African elephant's **habitat** is the forests and **savannas** south of the Sahara Desert. Flat, grassy savannas have plenty of plants for elephants to eat. Some African elephants live in an area called the bush. The bush lies between the savannas and forests. Elephants eat grasses that grow on the savanna. Then they rest in the shade of forest trees.

Asian elephants live in forests in Asia. Asian elephants eat plants that grow in forests. They also eat grasses that grow in open areas.

◄ Many elephants live in areas with plenty of trees.

What Elephants Eat

Elephants eat only plants. They eat grass, leaves, bark, shoots, flowers, and roots.

Elephants wander large areas of land to find food. Elephants walk more than 6,000 miles (9,700 kilometers) a year in search of food and water.

◀ Elephants rip off the tops of plants with their trunks.

The Life Cycle of an Elephant

Newborn calf

Calf

Juvenile

Male and female adults

Producing Young

Elephants live in **herds**. Herds can have up to 40 members. One female called the **matriarch** leads each herd. The matriarch is one of the oldest females in the herd. Adult male elephants are not part of the herd. They spend most of their time alone or in small groups with other male elephants.

Male and female elephants come together only to **mate.** A female elephant gives birth to a calf 22 months after mating.

Growing Up

An elephant calf drinks its mother's milk for up to six years. During these years, the calf learns how to use its trunk. It learns how to drink water and pull leaves off trees.

Calves take a long time to grow into adults. A male calf stays with its mother for the first 10 years of its life. A female elephant stays with its mother even after it becomes an adult. It joins the herd.

◄ Elephant calves learn to suck up water with their trunks and spray it into their mouths.

Dangers to Elephants

Elephants have few **predators**. Lions and tigers sometimes attack calves and sick elephants.

When a predator comes near, an elephant spreads its ears and twirls its trunk. If a herd is threatened, the matriarch stomps back and forth in front of the herd. The matriarch charges the predator to scare it away. Even though they're the largest land mammals, elephants still must protect themselves from predators.

◄ By spreading its ears, an elephant looks even bigger than it really is.

Amazing Facts about Elephants

- Elephants use their trunks to spray themselves with mud. The mud dries and protects their skin from the sun.
- The low noise elephants make can be heard by other elephants up to 5 miles (8 kilometers) away.
- Elephants often knock down trees in order to eat the leaves growing at the top.
- Elephants can live to be 70 years old.

◄ Elephants cannot sweat like people do. Elephants cool off in water and mud.

Glossary

habitat (HAB-uh-tat)—the place and natural conditions where an animal lives

herd (HURD)—a large group of animals that live together

mammal (MAM-uhl)—a warm-blooded animal that has a backbone; female mammals feed milk to their young.

mate (MAYT)—to join together to produce young

matriarch (MAY-tri-ark)—a female elephant that leads a herd; the matriarch often is the oldest elephant in the herd.

predator (PRED-uh-tur)—an animal that hunts other animals for food

savanna (suh-VAN-uh)—a large, flat area of grassland

warm-blooded (warm-BLUHD-id)—having a body temperature that stays the same

Read More

Dineen, Jacqueline. *Elephants.* Amazing Animals. Mankato, Minn.: Smart Apple Media, 2003.

Murray, Julie. *Elephants.* Animal Kingdom. Edina, Minn.: Abdo, 2003.

Internet Sites

FactHound offers a safe, fun way to find Internet sites related to this book. All of the sites on FactHound have been researched by our staff.

Here's how:
1. Visit *www.facthound.com*
2. Type in this special code **0736837175** for age-appropriate sites. Or enter a search word related to this book for a more general search.
3. Click on the **Fetch It** button.

FactHound will fetch the best sites for you!

Index